Tokyo. The world's larg... startlingly creative and rigorou... spotlessly organised and crazi... in ancient history and perpetu...

Everything imaginable is collected in one vertiginous metropolis: from a galaxy of Michelin stars to stellar street food, cosplay wackiness to catwalk winners, and pleasure services so left field they've even left the field.

But the dense metropolis has a quieter side in its alleyways and hidden corners. Its interiors hold a million surprises: a classy piano bar can be on the 8th floor above a fetish club, and heavenly yakiniku three floors below ground.

In a city with more than 80,000 restaurants a complete guide is impossible. But an insider's introduction will begin to unlock the wild mysteries of the Japanese capital.

Some local legends shared their side of the city: an arthouse filmmaker, the lady behind a famous fashion brand, a nightlife veteran and a top food critic. A feature exploring the vanished world of the yakuza is accompanied by an original short story from one of Japan's most successful writers. Get lost in the sights, sounds and flavours of the city. Get lost in Tokyo.

Photo: Uha

Odaiba is a man-made island in the Tokyo Bay, envisaged as the next boom town during the extravagant "Bubble Years" of the 1980s. It didn't quite materialise like that, but several huge developments have made the area worth visiting, not least the driverless Yurikamome train that takes you there. Dominating the skyline is the monumental *Fuji TV Building*. It was designed by postwar architectural legend Kenzo Tange, who took cues from modernism and Japanese traditions to help forge the movement called "metabolism".
• Fuji TV Building, Odaiba, Minato-ku

Tiny Art

Tokyo isn't the wild art paradise some might imagine. A rigid system requires most creators—or their reps—to pay in order to exhibit. But a few curators are shaking things up. In Daikanyama, The Container (pictured) is literally a shipping container, placed surreally inside a hair salon. The challenge is how each artist's work is curated into the space. This trend goes triple with *Tana Gallery Bookshelf*—a gallery literally on a shelf in a Jinbocho art school. Its curator has suggested that such extreme measures are required in order to maintain a truly independent art space in Tokyo.

• Various locations, see Index p.60

From Sea Grapes to Time Travel Gaming

Suntory Time

Food **Tropical Plunder**

Okinawa is one imperial colony Japan never gave back. But the former Ryukyu Kingdom's distinctive cuisine survives, and can be enjoyed in Tokyo. Typical dishes are "umibudo" (sea grapes)—seaweed bubbles that burst in your mouth, "champuru" stir-fry with bitter goya, soft-as-butter pork belly, and actual Spam. Options range from colourful greasy spoons to the fancy end: noisy, charming *Dachibin* (pictured; Koenji), ultra-refined *Akasaka Tantei* (Minato-ku), and *Awamori* (Ginza), which serves 150 types of the traditional liquor it's named after.

• Various locations, see Index p.60

Shop **Plastic Dreams**

In "Electric Town" Akihabara, the retro ideal of Japanese tech superiority lives on. From one-man specialist shops to massive outposts of the chains *Yamada Denki* and *Yodobashi Camera*, the only thing to stop you is voltage differences. "Akiba" is also capital of "otaku" (mega-fan) culture, where every geeky obsession has its expression. Maid cafés—cosplay-themed eateries—are ubiquitous and might leave you feeling a bit dirty. In manga bookshops you can find everything from cute animals to eye-watering hardcore—check out *Mandarake* for the full gamut. *Don Quijote* is a chaotic chain superstore with everything from robot toys and hi-tech air fresheners to knives, dried crabs and superhero costumes. The Akiba branch is notable as J-pop girl band AKB48 has its theatre upstairs. And *Akihabara Sega Gigo* is a good intro to gameland—from 1980s coin-slot machines in the basement to sprawling card-operated panels up top, it lets you time travel from the gaming past to its gleaming future.

• Akihabara, various locations, see Index p.60

Superb cuts and an emphasis on quality materials help make Tokyo a shopper's dream. For traditional with a twist, *Yuma Koshino* presents imaginative takes on classic Japanese garb, while *Yoshio Kubo* offers colourful tailored separates for men. *A Degree Fahrenheit* interprets Nipponese silhouettes minimalistically, with belted robes and roomy bottoms in muted tones. Hipster utilitarians should check out Hender Scheme's pared-down shop *Sukima* for shoes and leather goods to last. They'll match handcrafted denim from cult favourite Visvim, found in *F.I.L. Tokyo* or the Omotesando flagship *Visvim* store. At *Candy/Fake* (pictured), the collection goes from avant-garde to borderline bizarre, while at *Bape*, the sneakers might be iconic but you'll never forget the shop itself. Finally, concept stores *Graphpaper* and *See You Soon* have wildly different ways of showcasing local brands like White Mountaineering and Hombre Nino. One is stark and intellectual, the other like visiting a skateboard-loving friend.
• Various locations, see Index p.60

Culture | Dance of Darkness

The founders of the butoh dance movement worked in the postwar period to challenge the conservative scenes of Kabuki and Noh theatre. And their new form went on to influence contemporary dance worldwide. Famed company *Dairakudakan* (pictured) was founded by disciple Akaji Maro—who acted in "Kill Bill". Noted for letting young members develop original pieces, the troupe has its own theatre, where intimacy fuels a powerful voyage through humour, titillation, uneasiness and awe.
• Dairakudakan Kochuten, Kichijoji, dairakudakan.com

Food · Night **Six Trees**

Roppongi has its critics, thanks to touts, strip clubs and trashy discos. But Tokyo's nightlife hub has something for every taste. See avant-garde arts space *SuperDeluxe*—with something extraordinary happening most evenings. Expect line-ups of outlandish musicians, DJs analogue mixing with tape decks, architectural slideshows or sound-and-light experiments. An upscale dinner spot is *Warayakiya*, where burning straw is used to heat food at 900°C—meaning your blood-red chunks of "katsuo" (skipjack tuna) are perfectly seared on the outside, while raw inside. For a different sustenance, all comers are welcome—during 24 hours—at *Chinese Café Eight* (pictured)—a warm, buzzing eatery decorated with sex organs of all types including a giant, golden phallus—bound to make anyone crave some crispy duck.

• Roppongi, various locations, see Index p.60

Food **Holy Mackerel**

Izakayas lie between bars and restaurants, involving multiple small dishes and copious late-night guzzling of beer, sake and shochu. They range from crazily cheap chains where all dishes are 270 yen and there's an all-you-can-drink option, to gourmet, high-end offerings. *Shirube* sits perfectly on the spectrum, thanks to a rambunctious atmosphere, exquisite fusion menu—and sake served in ice-cold bamboo tubes. There are a few branches, but the Shimokitazawa one provides a good platform for exploring that neighbourhood. You'll leave wondering why all edamame isn't fried in chilli and garlic, and the memory of the blowtorched mackerel (pictured) will tingle on your tongue for days.

• Shirube, Shimokitazawa

Zen grew up in New Zealand and was en route to becoming a chef, when a stopover in the hometown of his parents changed his plans. In Tokyo he set off on a new path: having working for a key Japanese footwear brand he's now engaged in marketing for fragrance label retaW

Zen Tsujimoto, Fashion Professional

Coming Home

When Zen fell in love with Tokyo he immersed himself metaphorically in the vibrant fashion and club scene—and literally in the city's public baths. He parts the warm vapours to reveal the charms of faded Mount Fuji murals—and plenty of shopping, clubbing and lazing tips too

How did you get into the Tokyo fashion world?

Actually it was an accident—my background in New Zealand was in cooking. I was on my way to France to pursue a culinary career but stopped in Japan for a couple of months. It was then I realised I had no idea about my own culture. So, I never got on the plane to France. As a young kid I was interested in style, so Tokyo seemed a good chance to try out a different medium and begin my career in fashion.

What's your neighbourhood—and why is it unique?

Currently, Nakano. It's nice, down-beat and has a lot of great places to eat. It's a small stretch from work and less refined than Omotesando—but it's nice to have a contrast to my workplace. There's also *Nakano Broadway*, a building complex stacked with tons of vintage gems. I've moved several times in Tokyo —I've enjoyed living in different areas. It gives you a new outlook on the city which is healthy.

What do you most look forward to in Tokyo, when you've been away?

The food, the high level of service and the general cleanliness of every-thing. The ordinary things you can easily take for granted when you get caught up in daily life. I've also developed withdrawal symptoms from rice and miso soup.

What do you like to do on your own?

After a big weekend, I often go to the local "sento" (public bathhouse) to sweat it out. I was never a huge fan of baths as a kid, but I enjoy a good session now. Submerged under the hot water, the intense heat washes away your hangover. You feel like a new person. One of my favourites is *Chiyo-no-yu*. It's the local public bathhouse, five minutes from my place. It feels like another

time period as you step through the "noren" curtains, because the place was built in 1951. It's spacious and never crowded because it's in the suburbs—sometimes I get the whole place to myself. There's a big mural of Mount Fuji to simulate an outdoor onsen—tacky but charming.

For a more refined experience, try *Shimizu-yu* sento. It's over 100 years old, but was refurbished in 2009. It's a lot bigger and right in the centre—shops like Comme Des Garçons and Yohji Yamamoto are a short walk away. Don't be put off by the fancy interior—it's still only 4 60 yen entry, and an extra 1,000 yen for the sauna. Nearby there's a good soba joint, *Aoyama Kawakami-An*, for a post-bath meal. If it's a nice day, the third floor has a balcony.

How is the club scene?

Pretty good. I'd say most nights inevitably end up in Shibuya as it hosts most of the best gigs. *Sound Museum Vision*, *Unit*, *Womb*, *Sankeys*... Most of these places literally go several floors under-ground. There's also a pretty good live-record scene with bars like *Grandfather's* and *JBS*. *DJ Bar Bridge* sometimes plays vinyl too.

And your favourite place outside of a bar or club?

The back gardens of *Nezu Museum*. There's a beautiful garden out the back that largely goes unnoticed. It's so peaceful and quiet that it makes you forget you're in the middle of Aoyama.

Is high-priced Tokyo still good for sub-cultural movements?

It's a common misconception that Tokyo is high-priced. Sure, like any big city the rent can be expensive, but if you know where to find value the cost of living is a lot cheaper than cities like New York or London. It also has something to do with

Mori Art Museum offers high-profile exhibitions as well as a stunning view of the sprawl up top, from Tokyo City View

United Arrows
Shibuya

Beams
Shibuya

Isetan
Shinjuku

Idea By Sosu
Omotesando

F.I.L. Tokyo
Omotesando

G.I.P Store
Shibuya

Paradise Tokyo
Nakameguro

Mister Hollywood
Omotesando

Yaeca Home Store
Minato-ku

Tokyo City View
Roppongi

New York Bar
Shinjuku-ku

Narisawa
Minato-ku

**Sushidokoro
Shintanaka**
Meguro-ku

Yogoro
Shibuya-ku

Shinjuku Gyoen
Shinjuku

Yoyogi Park
Harajuku

the stigma of Japanese food being high-end and expensive overseas. In terms of subcultural movements, Nakameguro is home to a new generation of upcoming designers with their own stores, like *Markaware*, Nonnative's flagship store *Vendor* and *Wacko Maria*. Local brand Sasquatchfabrix doesn't have its own store, but is carried at Japanese retailers like *United Arrows* and *Beams*. The designer Daisuke Yokoyama has a solid design philosophy and his process comes from a deep place of creativity. He's quite forward-thinking and progressive, and was mixing traditional Japanese silhouettes with a contemporary style before it became fashionable. Another young design duo is Almostblack (Shunta Nakajima and Masaki Kawase)— find their stuff at boutiques like the Men's department at Isetan, and *Idea By Sosu* in Omotesando Hills.

What are five words that describe your personal fashion style?
  Simple. Subdued. Sentimental. Practical. Functional.

Where can we buy this style in Tokyo?
  Visvim brand at *F.I.L. Tokyo*, WTAPS at *G.I.P Store*, *Paradise Tokyo*, N.Hoolywood at *Mister Hollywood* and *Yaeca Home Store*. Yaeca, in my opinion, is a very slept-on brand with such a great sense of simple style and elegance in the products— from unique shirting to loose-cut trousers, both for men and women.

What is your favourite place to watch over the city?
  Tokyo City View at the Mori Tower is 238 metres high and has a 360-degree view. On a clear day you can see the urban sprawl as far as the eye can see. It gives you an idea of the immensity of the city. *The New York Bar* on the 52nd floor of The Park Hyatt is famous from "Lost In Translation".

Could you share your favourite restaurants too?
  Narisawa has got to be one of the best culinary experiences I've ever had. I was lucky enough to be treated to lunch one day. It was like eating art. The tastes, the textures, the concept of every dish was just sensory overload. It also supposedly has one of the most sustainable culinary practices. I've heard the waiting list can be up to one month.
  Shintanaka is a very small sushi counter that sits about ten people, in a residential area called Toritsu Daigaku. Ever since the documentary "Jiro Dreams of Sushi", everyone seems to think there's only one place for sushi. But if you can find Shintanaka, and go with a Japanese speaker, you'll find much lower prices and amazing quality.
  The curry at *Yogoro* is sensational. There's only a few options on the menu but the popular choice is a spinach chicken curry topped with a poached egg and melted cheese. Nishi the owner-chef used to be editor-in-chief of "Boon Magazine", and decided one day to cook curry. So he taught himself through YouTube. Lunchtimes are packed.

Any favourite public recreation area?
  Shinjuku Gyoen. Yoyogi Park is nice in its own way too—it has a lot of character—but Shinjuku Gyoen makes you quickly forget you are in one of earth's most populated places by the sheer size of the beautifully maintained park. It's also usually less crowded than Yoyogi Park which makes for a peaceful place to read a book or hang out with friends.

Which areas are best to explore Tokyo by walking or biking?
  First-timers should start in Shibuya then head over to Daikanyama, Nakameguro and Ebisu.
  Daikanyama T-Site has an impressive selection of books and

Japanese furniture from the modern era is displayed in uncharacteristically spacious digs, at Pacific Furniture Service

magazines. Down the road is a 1919-built Japanese-style house that survived WWII and the earth-quake—*Kyu Asakura House*. It costs almost nothing to get in. Lovely place to take a book and sit on the tatami mats overlooking the garden.

Just down the hill is Nakameguro. A beautiful canal runs through it dotted with tons of nice shops and cafés, parallel to the Yamanote line tracks. The whole river also explodes in pink during springtime because it's lined with sakura trees.

In Ebisu check *Pacific Furniture Service*, with mid-century Japanese furniture. The interior is really nice—it's rare to see a shop of this size in Tokyo. An extra store around the back specialises in tools and stationery. *Post* is another great bookstore in Ebisu. They also do the curation for the space in *Dover Street Market* in Ginza.

Tokyo is blessed with many great museums. Which are your favourites?

The National Art Center. When I saw the Issey Miyake retrospective I was left wanting to go back many more times. The building itself is also beautiful. *Mori Art Museum* continuously has good exhibitions, as well as the killer view from its roof. *Kawamura Memorial DIC Museum of Art* is probably my favourite but takes two hours to get there from the city. It has an extensive collection, and even a permanent Rothko room. But the best is the huge hydrangea garden which is unbeatable in summer.

Left Field

From Nakano to Mitaka along the JR Chuo train line lie several one-time havens of 1960s counterculture that retain a singular vibe today. Ride west of Shinjuku and get lost in each area's distinct personality

Food · Night   Music for the Mouth

Some spots have escaped Tokyo's relentless construction to preserve reminders of earlier epochs. On prime real estate across from Kichijoji station, *Harmonica Yokocho* is a scruffy anomaly amid rapid gentrification. This cluster of covered alleyways started out as a postwar black market, and retains its bygone feel—though occupants have mostly moved with the times. The ten-seat counter at Kataguchi feels like dining with your own personal sushi chef, and a kushiyaki meal at Niwatori is as intimate. The scene is lively at ramshackle corner bar Kopanda or Eihire—a roomier standing bar across the street. Groups should try Tecchan (pictured), where the counter surrounds a large kitchen serving yakitori and other essentials. And it's worth queuing at Minmin, which has served plump gyoza and ramen since the 1970s.
• Harmonica Yokocho, Kichijoji

Shelf Fillers

Fashionable types grumbling that Harajuku has lost its edge have found a haven in Koenji, among a network of over 100 used clothing shops. Most stores are found on the south side of the station, and you could spend a whole afternoon searching for the perfect getup. Try *Suntrap* for classy vintage US menswear, or *Hikari* and *Spank!* for ultra-girly 1980s styles. The "inspirational vintage" selections at *Sokkyou* (pictured) have earned it a cult following, while if you want something really outlandish, the extravagantly remodelled clothes at *Hayatochiri*, in the anarchic Kitakore Building, are unlikely to disappoint.
• Koenji, various locations, see Index p.60

Culture **Speakers Corner**

Back in the 1950–60s, few people in Japan could afford a large record collection. So they went to dedicated cafés, "meikyoku kissa", to get their fix. One of few surviving examples, *Violon* resembles a miniature Viennese music hall, where customers sit in respectful silence as classical music wafts from nearly century-old speakers. It's a sanctuary from Tokyo life, and—unlike at most other meikyoku kissa—the coffee is drinkable. Live music recitals occur almost every evening, and if you get hungry, the same owners' Thai restaurant next door is excellent.
• Violon, 2-9-5 Asagaya,
meikyoku-kissa-violon.com

Culture · Night **Live Wires**

Decorated in psychedelic red-on-black swirls, *UFO Club* is a good place to catch the elder statesmen of Japan's underground rock scene and some of their younger disciples. At *Niman Denatsu*—Japanese for "20,000 volts"—the music skews more towards punk and hardcore, with the sound system cranked punishingly loud. These two venues are in Higashi (East) Koenji, but the whole neighbourhood is famed for its live music scene and spectrum of venues. Back in central Koenji, look out for events at *Sound Studio Dom*, a rehearsal studio on the main shopping arcade that also hosts informal DIY gigs.
• Koenji, various locations, see Index p.60

Swan About

When the cherry trees bloom, few places are as picturesque as *Inokashira Park*. Centred around a long, narrow pond, the green space is disarmingly attractive at any time of year, and it draws a weekend crowd to match. If you're tempted to rent one of the swan-shaped pedal boats, be warned: local legend says any couple who ventures out will break up, thanks to a jealous goddess enshrined by the water. The park is also home to a small zoo, and continues west to the world-beloved animation studio's *Ghibli Museum*, where advance reservations are essential.
• Inokashira Park, Kichijoji; Ghibli Museum, Kichijoji, ghibli-museum.jp

Shop **Monsters' Mall**

The early 2000s saw mainstream acceptance of "otaku", anime and manga fans once considered outcasts. And 1960s shopping mall *Nakano Broadway* duly bore a gradual colonisation by geeks. The ground floor still maintains a veneer of normality, while upstairs a warren of shops cater to every nerdy passion. Collectible figurines are the biggest draw, plus everything from pro-wrestler masks and model cars to Care Bears and Game & Watch consoles. Otaku can also rent out cases to display their own wares, offering a public window into some very private obsessions.
• Nakano Broadway, Nakano, nbw.jp/index_e.html

Shop **Slipped Discs**

Anyone who feels there's nothing new under the musical sun should make a pilgrimage to this bastion of esoterica. *Los Apson?* owner Keiji Yamabe was a buyer at legendary Roppongi shop Wave—sadly no more—and has deep ties with the Tokyo music underground. His selection of CDs and new and used LPs ranges from Latin imports to obscure psychedelia, field recordings, harsh noise—Merzbow fans, take note—and CD-Rs and mixtapes by obscure Japanese DJs and bands. Other Tokyo record shops may have larger stocks, but none are as single-mindedly devoted to the weird and wilfully uncommercial.
• Los Apson?, Koenji, losapson.net

Food | **Ko-Kreation**

You'll lose count of how many people you see carrying musical instruments through the streets of Koenji. And many of them will join impromptu busking jams under the bridges late into the night, making it a good reason to stick around until well after the sun goes down. Just grabbing beers from the "conbini" and sitting in the north- or south-side squares is a perfectly respectable way to pass the time. But with its eclectic, arty residents, the thriving neighbourhood has plenty else to keep you there after all the local vintage shops have closed doors for the night. Not least a network of yakitori shops clustered around the railway tracks. *Taisho* is the most famous, and has

three restaurants where the seating—stools and beer-crate tables—spills out onto the pavement during warmer months. *Tonkichi*, another popular spot, specialises in "yakiton" (grilled pork skewers). For a retro experience, order the "hoppy set": a DIY cocktail of shochu liquor served with low-alcohol beer substitute—that's the "hoppy" bit—to mix yourself. Wander into the tunnels under the tracks to find a host of other mini eateries and bars... Or walk up the various "shotengai"—pedestrianised shopping streets, and allow your senses to create your own itinerary.
• Koenji, various locations, see Index p.60

Miwa Nishikawa, Filmmaker
Real Connection

One of Japan's most exciting—
and few female—independent
filmmakers, Miwa started off
as assistant director to Cannes
veteran filmmaker Hirokazu
Koreeda before forging
her own path. She recently
completed her fifth feature film
"The Long Excuse"

**Mysterious middle-aged men eat at humble izakayas, and a hot pot
dish favoured by sumo wrestlers makes for a good hangover cure...
The kind, friendly personality of Tokyo—as seen through Miwa's
lens—conflicts with the yearning for close relationships in this
many-layered metropolis**

Photo: Julia Shiki

How has Tokyo influenced your work?

The protagonist of "The Long Excuse" is a novelist who lives in Tokyo with his wife. He is quite well off, living large in a stylish neighborhood. However, he doesn't have much of a connection with people around him. Tokyo is a place where you can easily live in solitude if you choose. Despite the fact that there are so many people, buildings, and different groups, you can detach yourself from others by choice.

Which areas have you lived in?

I used to live in a small apartment in Nakano ward when I was a student at Waseda University and commuted on the Tozai line. It's a big but folksy town, not so stylish but has the common touch. I moved near Gotokuji station on the Odakyu line after starting my film career. It's still a small town with mom-and-pop stores. I've also lived near Shimotakaido station on the Keio line. I currently live in an area near the border of Suginami and Setagaya wards. It is small and doesn't even have a restaurant to dine in during the night. Because I am originally from Hiroshima, I tend to prefer smaller neighbourhoods because it feels more like home. In fact I like areas considered a bit uncool or unsophisticated.

Your films show a keen understanding of human nature: where are good places for people watching?

Some people do say I am a sharp observer of human behaviour but I don't just watch people, especially if they are complete strangers. There are just too many people in Tokyo for that. However, I do often get inspiration from people close to me. Often while drinking, people tell me about their troubles in life. I use these to come up with descriptions of characters or ideas for my work.

You depicted the feel of an izakaya in "Dreams for Sale"—can you name some izakayas you go to regularly?

Tokyo is full of them. I often go into an ordinary izakaya that isn't stylish or anything. Because my office is in Shibuya, my coworkers and I often go to a 24-hour izakaya, *Yamaga Honten*. During the day, you often find middle-aged men— you have no idea what they do for a living. When we finish at an irregular time we go in for a drink. However, with my female friends, we'd go to a nicer place, like *Potsura-potsura* in Shinsen. It's a restaurant that serves sake in a wine glass. The seafood and vegetable dishes are delicious.

What are your favourite types of food and where do you eat them?

My favourite foods are natto (fermented soy beans) and mutton. I have Mongolian mutton barbecue—we call it "Genghis Khan"—at a counter restaurant called *Darumaya* in Shinjuku. I have friends in Nakameguro so we often eat around there as well. A Singaporean restaurant called *Five Star Cafe* serves good chicken rice. *Shibamatsu* is great for hot pot. I go there often to eat "chankonabe" —a hotpot typically eaten by sumo wrestlers—when I'm hungover.

Which art galleries do you like?

Art history was my major but I barely studied nor do I go see art much. The most recent was the "shunga" (erotic art) exhibition at the *Eisei Bunko Museum*. It wasn't an ideal environment though because it was so jam-packed.

Which Tokyo-based films do you like?

I am uneasy about saying this because director Hirokazu Koreeda is my mentor, but I really like his film "Nobody Knows". It was released more than ten years ago but still captures the characteristics of Tokyo. For example how human relationships can be almost nonexistent. People aren't aware how their next-door neighbours live their lives. The city's skyscrapers and luxury lifestyle are not shown in the film but it still has a very Tokyo feel to it. Another more recent movie I enjoyed was "Shin-Gozilla". Tokyo is a metropolis worthy of destroying. It was exciting to watch.

Do you go to see live music?
I like indie music. I don't go to huge concert halls but small venues in Koenji. Some of the musicians I listen to are R&B band More Rhythm, female jazz quartet Zukunasi, and guitarist Takehara Pistol who also acted in my film "The Long Excuse". I go to see bands from other regions like The Takosan from Osaka, when they come to Tokyo. I go to *Blue Note* every few years because it's pricy.

If you could make Tokyo a better place, what would you change?
That would be to make the city a better place for children. It would be ideal if parents could send their kids somewhere safe during work. Kids can't play outside freely. It's sad. I wish Tokyo would listen to the voices of children. When we shoot in the countryside, random children greet us. This never happens in Tokyo. It's as if kids in the city are living inside a vast space of distrust. The solution is not as simple as increasing nurseries. It would be ideal if a regional community could look after children, perhaps couples without kids or elderly people with free time.
Another thing would be to make shooting films easier. It's very difficult to get approval at most locations. For example, in the subway. In "Dreams for Sale", set in Tokyo, we had to shoot at a subway

in Chiba. In other parts of the country people welcome us because it promotes their town and leads to revitalisation, but in Tokyo we're a nuisance. Giant monster movies are filmed here only because they are backed up by the Ministry of Defense. I wish we could shoot films like they do in New York City and Paris.

If you had a friend from abroad visiting Tokyo, what would you do?
A boat ride in Ichigaya, or a party on a traditional "yakata" boat would be nice. I live in west Tokyo so I'd recommend *Daikanyama T-Site*. Or if the weather is nice, a picnic in *Shinjuku Gyoen*. You can't bring alcohol inside the park, but we'd buy a lunchbox at *Isetan* department store. The *Showa Memorial Park* in Tachikawa is a good place to go in spring and early summer. My friends and I started a hiking club and we recently climbed *Mount Takao*. It's perfect if you never hiked before. It's definitely a convenient mountain for city people, with many restaurants along the path.
In terms of dining, there's everything you can think of. You can eat foods from around the world and they are usually high quality. I've been recently frequenting *Le Lion*—a French bistro in Ebisu. Someone raised in Paris recommended it to me. We go there when we have something to celebrate. We shot a scene there for my film too. In terms of sushi, I sometimes go when treated because I wouldn't be able to afford it by myself. It's the best part of going to a sushi bar. But there is one sushi restaurant in Ebisu called *Sushi Matsue* where I've been a regular. Masahiro Yasuda, the late producer, took me there after my debut film. It's very small, not overly expensive and serves delicious sushi. If you are in the mood for meat, *Matsukiya*

Get perspective just 50 minutes from Shinjuku on top of Mount Takao—take a picnic or a grab a soba at a local place

serves good sukiyaki and shabu-shabu. It's not large but there's a "zashiki" (tatami area) to relax on. We go there when we feel like good meat. *Sato* in Nishi-Azabu is good for "kappo" fine dining. It branched off from a soba shop in Hiroo. Sato-san the head chef prepares seasonal seafood and vegetables delicately in small portions and serves soba to round off the meal. I dine at these nicer restaurants when someone treats me. Otherwise I am happy with the 24-hour izakaya.

If Tokyo was a character in a film, what would it be like?
That is a difficult question because Tokyo's demography is actually more diverse than you might imagine. It's not just businessmen in suits and glasses. Personally I like Tokyo very much

because it's full of strangers. Most people are from outside. But original Tokyoites rarely reject or make fun of them. Other cities in Japan are not as open. Sapporo and Fukuoka are also comfortable, but not as diverse. In Tokyo, people from across the nation and world live and work together. It's wonderful. Because there is not much of a psychological wall between the people, they can be tolerant and kind to each other. But generally, at heart, most people feel lonely. Since everyone uses a common language, it's difficult to know how much people truly understand each other on a deeper level. So, Tokyo as a character is a kind and friendly person who could be involved with many people... But it's hard to know with how many he or she feels a real connection.

Where Have all the Yakuza Gone?

Jake Adelstein

If you want to see the yakuza of Japan stroll down neon-lit backstreets in black and white suits, with tattoos showing at the edge of their sleeves, and the occasional shoot-out or swordfight—well, you're going to need to invest in a PlayStation and a copy of Sega's "Yakuza Zero". That's as close as you'll get to those long-gone days.

This year there was a very public brawl—between members of the Yamaguchi-gumi and splinter group Kobe Yamaguchi-gumi. It was a throw-back to "the good old" days. No one had seen anything like it in years.

Japan's mafia exists in a strange grey zone of legality. They are regulated but not banned. There are 22 Designated Organised Crime groups subject to especially tough law enforcement. The largest, the Yamaguchi-gumi, has been in business since 1915. It's nine years older than Toyota.

The three largest groups are like corporations. They have a board of directors, management committees, and all the lower-tier groups pay a franchise fee upwards.

The Yamaguchi-gumi's diamond symbol is as well-known as the Golden Arches of McDonald's here. Every group has headquarters, with the address listed on the National Police Agency site. The Inagawakai still has an office across from the Ritz Carlton. You have to climb some stairs to get there. I don't suggest you do, and if you do, don't tell them I sent you.

In 1999, when I was a police reporter for the "Yomiuri Shimbun", I was assigned to cover Shinjuku's fourth district, which houses Kabukicho—Tokyo's legendary red-light district.

Over a hundred yakuza groups had offices in the narrow area. The de-militarised zone was a sprawling, dimly lit, smoky coffee shop called The Parisienne. The menu included Mont-Blanc, a chestnut cream-cake invented in France, but that was about as French as it got.

The café faced Kuyakusho Street, running through the centre of Kabukicho. It is about 100 metres north of the Shinjuku local city hall. Restaurants, bars, rip-off bars, host clubs and adult entertainment joints occupied that block. It was located in the Furinkaikan building, literally the "The Wind and Forest Hall", which had six floors. It housed a sauna, a nightclub, a yakuza front company, a pawnshop, and The Parisienne.

Walking in there was like walking into a strangely laid-out open office. The lights were dim halogen and the lounge chairs mostly velvet. Islands of tables were mashed together with fuzzy sofas marking off territories. This was where local yakuza came to meet, snack, talk business or shit to each other and their rivals. For "yakuza-watching", it was the place.

It had an aura of tension, excitement, melancholy and danger, mingled with jazz on the speakers.

I once saw a middle-aged yakuza literally throw his finger at a man I assumed was his boss. It rolled out of the white handkerchief onto the floor. One of the bellboys chased after it while the angry middle-aged yakuza yelled, waving around his hand, with a short finger neatly wrapped in white gauze. There wasn't a bloody stump to stare at. The finger was found, wrapped up, and quietly put back on the table by the bellboy.

No one tips in Japan but he probably should have been tipped.

There were shootings there before I became a reporter. In the hot summer of 1990, a junior member of the Sumiyoshikai shot to death a banished former boss of the same organisation. The victim Yoshiharu Kimura, who dressed and acted like a businessman, had muscled in on the gang's territory even after getting kicked out. The killer fired while nearly a hundred people were in the café. Chaos ensued.

The shooter turned himself in a few days later, with a gun carrying two bullets, and was immediately arrested on violations of the sword and firearms control act. Later he was re-arrested for murder.

Shootings weren't so rare in the 1990s. The police used to joke, "What crime is it when a yakuza kills another yakuza?" The punchline: "Destruction of property."

The next shooting in the café took place in 2002. I followed the case for the Yomiuri. One October evening, a little past 7pm, it was reported that "gunshots had been fired". Two Chinese gangsters shot two Sumiyoshikai executive members with a handgun. Kazuo Shiraishi, an underboss, aged 36, bled to death from four gunshot wounds. His buddy survived.

The shooters were from Shanghai and were said to have had a conversation with the other two that soon escalated into an argument. Witnesses reporting overhearing: "That is not what we discussed."

At one point, Shiraishi allegedly put his gun on the table and said, "You think you can kill me? Try it."

Apparently, one of the Chinese gangsters tried, and Shiraishi died. The incident was widely reported because it fed into paranoia about "foreign mobs" taking over Japan. It's a myth the cops perpetuate to keep budgets high, and the mobsters to justify their existence. "Better the enemy that you know…", the yakuza would argue.

The Chinese gangs in Kabukicho were always a minor force. A few raids by immigration after the incident pretty much wiped out "the Chinese mafia". The legend lives on.

Where have all the Chinese mafia gone? Back to China.

What was the cause of the 2002 dispute? There are theories galore.

The most credible source I knew claimed it was over kickbacks on sales of stolen goods the Chinese thugs were procuring from break-ins, muggings and armed robberies. That was probably the case.

You see, there's the essential difference between yakuza and the common criminal—at least it was in the old days. Yakuza didn't steal, rob, or engage in petty theft. It was one reason they were sort of tolerated.

Kenji Sakurai, a Yamaguchi-gumi boss who retired in 2013, explains it like this.

"After the war, Japan was in chaos. All the Korean and Taiwanese slave labourers of Imperial Japan were free and the [US Occupiers] made them untouchable by Japanese police. So they took over black markets and ran amuck. The yakuza—which were gambler federations, right wing groups or street merchant associations before the war—became a second police force.

"We took the street gangs, the thugs, the foreigners, the half-breeds and gave them discipline. A code of honor. You joined the yakuza, you got a family. We gave you work, purpose, and guidance. However, street crime was always bad—bad for our image and for businesses on our turf—so no theft, no mugging, none of that."

Fencing stolen goods was frowned on as well.

"Nowadays, yakuza will do anything to make money. Lie, cheat, mug and steal. Sell drugs. It's all gone to shit."

Sakurai longs for the days when yakuza made money the honorable way: racketeering, loan sharking, evicting people and collecting debts.

Laws and time have not been kind to the yakuza. For years numbers stayed close to 80,000 but in October 2011, new organised crime ordinances went into effect nationwide. These laws made it illegal to pay off yakuza or financially benefit them. It was revolutionary but effective: the person who uses the yakuza or gives into them is also a criminal.

It also forced companies to put anti-yakuza clauses in contracts. In simple terms, if a yakuza wants to rent an apartment, borrow a car, join a gym or get a cellphone, he has to sign a contract that he's not a member of an organised crime group. Of course, if he signs, that's a lie. So he may be able to join the gym, but the police can now arrest him for fraud.

And the cops do it all the time. If you're a tattooed man, you can't even rent a hotel room without risking arrest.

It ain't easy to make a dishonest living without a phone, apartment, or bank account. The only places that will openly hire yakuza are the nuclear facilities still dotting Japan. In the recent documentary, "Yakuza And The Constitution", some older thugs lament they're being deprived of basic human rights. The police argument is always: "if you want human rights, leave the yakuza and join the human race."

Yep.

Numbers have dropped to below 46,000. More than half are "associate members". These are sworn-in mobsters who obscure their identity. In other words, they don't show their faces in the yakuza fan magazines.

Numbers keep dwindling and those who remain are getting older. The median age is close to 55. The yakuza rarely shoot each other anymore or anyone else. It's too dangerous and too expensive.

Under Japan's severe gun control laws not only is having a gun a crime, having a gun with bullets that match it is another, and firing the gun, yet another. Fire a gun, go to jail for life. That's too dangerous for old yakuza who don't want to die in jail.

Yakuza have only recently been held criminally responsible for the actions of their subordinates, but in civil court, since 2007, "employer liability" is routinely applied to make yakuza pay for the damage their soldiers commit. In 2012, boss Tadamasa Goto had to pay the equivalent of 1.4 million dollars to the family of a man his thugs had killed.

Because bosses don't want to pay damages, they discourage their thugs from committing violent acts. This makes people less afraid and more willing to go to the police. It makes extortion money very hard to collect.

Hideaki Kubori, a lawyer who specialises in dealing with organised crime, says, "There's no need for the yakuza anymore. There are more lawyers now and we have taken over most of the jobs they used to do."

Debt collection? Lawyers. Evicting tenants? Lawyers.

Who needs yakuza?

Where have all the yakuza gone?

Possibly some of the smarter ones went to law school. A lot commit suicide. Many wind up in jail.

But where can you see them?

They're not in Paris and they're not in The Parisienne.

The whole café was closed and redecorated in 2003. It reopened in 2004, brightly lit, with less than half the floor space.

You can visit it if you like. Sometimes, late at night, you'll see an old yakuza stumble in, out of habit, or in a drunken stupor. Maybe he's just out of prison after a long stretch and is looking for his old buddies.

Where have all the yakuza gone?

They're hiding in office buildings or crappy apartments serving as make-shift offices. These days, they're even forced to share offices with other gangsters from different groups. They don't wear their badges. The newbies don't get tattoos.

The young yakuza today—there aren't many—don't chop off fingers and beg forgiveness when they quit; they send a politely worded email.

You can find the remaining yakuza in the fanzines and maybe if you stand outside their offices, you might spot them coming and going.

The yakuza in Tokyo. They're like the payphone booths you still see in a few parts of the city. Barely used, aging badly, outdated, not making much money, but still standing.

At least the phone booths are useful.

Jake Adelstein has been a crime journalist in Japan since 1993. He is the managing editor of Japan Subculture Research Center

Like the phoenix of the Tokyo
club scene, Yuko has worked
defining one legendary city
club after another. Her storied
career behind the scenes has
included booking for fabled
venue Space Lab Yellow, along
with Eleven and Air. Mid-2016
saw her co-found new Shibuya
dance palace Contact, where
she can usually be found today

Yuko Ichikawa, Promoter

Setting the Tone

The constantly morphing Tokyo nightclub scene is accompanied by tiny music bars stuffed with records, afterparties under a cherry tree and plenty of places to find sustenance on the way—from tuna heads to a cosy hot pot in a restaurant frequented by techno DJs. Yuko turns up the volume on her city nightscape

What is hot in Tokyo at the moment?

There's been a boom in dance-oriented Japanese bands. One reason is the younger generation is more into open-air festivals these days—they don't like clubbing so much. I'm in my forties and people of my generation had a great time in clubs in the 1990s, so we still like partying. Now younger people are more conservative. They probably just buy cheap booze and drink it at home with friends.

Where's the district to be these days?

Let's say Shibuya because I'm working there now. When I first came to Tokyo to study, I came from Matsumoto in Nagano Prefecture. That's like countryside and at first I found the Shibuya crowds too overwhelming. Now it's also lost its cool fashion edge because of all the fast-fashion shops. But as my club Contact is there, I spend a lot of time there. It's actually a great spot for clubs because it's really convenient for transport, and all kinds of crowds come through.

You booked for some great Tokyo clubs in the past, like Space Lab Yellow, but they sadly closed down. How come?

With Yellow, the building owner sold it, and the new owner wanted to sell it again for a higher price, so he asked us to move out. But they couldn't sell the building, so we opened the club Eleven in the same place. However, then, the building owner decided he could make more money running a commercial club by himself, so he kicked us out. He tried four different clubs in that space and every one failed. With the club Air it was different, in that location it wasn't possible to get the Fueiho law license. This is a law from 1948 that prohibited all-night dancing in many venues. It's now

finally been changed. But because of that the owner decided to sell Air and open a new club with a legal license, and that is Contact.

So can you tell us a bit about your club now?

Contact is on Dogenzaka street in Shibuya. It's in the basement of a carpark—you'd never imagine there could be a club in such a place. The dancefloor is reminiscent of Yellow. So, we're trying to give people an old and new feeling. We're trying to book up-and-coming talents and also pass down good music to a younger generation. So, we go from things like Nicky Siano and a Paradise Garage tribute night to new artists like Huerco S, Call Super, Discodromo, Northern Electronics, Giegling and so on.

Who are some interesting acts from Japan at the moment?

DJ Nobu is getting popular outside Japan, and he's leading Tokyo's techno scene right now. Wata Igarashi is a good producer and is putting effort into DJing too. On the house scene I'd say Keita Sano, who performs live. Ryo Murakami also performs live, and recently won the silver prize at the Venice Music Biennale. On the art side, Ummmi is super interesting. She's still a student at Tokyo University of the Arts but I'm very interested in her work. I've been thinking of asking her to make a video installation at our club.

Apart from clubs—are there interesting live-music venues to check out?

I don't have much time these days but I love to listen to real live music at *Blue Note*. I went there for Chucho Valdes, Femi Kuti and Pat Metheny, to name a few.

WWW X just opened. I haven't been there yet, but I'm keen to check it out. It used to be a

Besides its gleaming towers, Tokyo is filled with alleyways like Shibuya's Nonbei Yokocho, where izakaya Kibi is found

Oath
Shibuya

DJ Bar Bridge
Shibuya

JBS
Shibuya

Little Soul Café
Setagaya-ku

Tractor
Nakameguro

cinema—I remember watching films there in my twenties. I'd wake up early and go to the first screenings to avoid the line. Now it's been revived as a live venue with soundproofed walls, and a Funktion-One sound system.

If we're still not tired after a night out, what should we do?

If you still want to party, *Oath* is where everyone goes for the afterparty. I think the door charge is almost free, the first drink is 1,000 yen, and then all drinks are 500 yen each. So it's no fuss to go even if you don't know who's playing. The staff are nice and you can listen to good, local Djs. There's also a cherry tree outside, so it's lovely to have drinks outside from spring to autumn.

Outside of clubs—which bars are good for music lovers?

Our company runs *DJ Bar Bridge*, on the tenth floor looking right down on the famous Shibuya crossing. It has weekly or biweekly resident DJs and only charges 1,000 yen entry including a drink. A great bar I'd love to go to is *JBS*. It's near my club but it closes early so I've never made it. In Shimokitazawa there's a great music bar called *Little Soul Café*. It's an upstairs place that has shelves with thousands of records. If you ask the owner for any track, he always has it—which is always surprising! I've been a few times with DJs, to listen to good tunes and talk about music.

Another favourite bar is *Tractor* —it's a small place in Nakameguro. The owners used to have a bar called Combine just near the

Meguro River, where Richie Hawtin, Steve Bug and many DJs used to visit to have ten drinks or more. I was never able to leave that place after a couple of drinks—I always ended up staying till they closed up. A very dangerous place, but I loved it. When they had to move out they started Tractor. So all the regulars go there now instead.

Can you mention good places to eat?
A friend of mine owns a small izakaya called *Kibi*. It's in Nonbei Yokocho, a little alleyway in Shibuya. She used to work in the industry so there's often a lot of techno DJs eating in the restaurant. You do the typical izakaya experience there—drinking shochu and sharing many small dishes. They sometimes make "nabe" (hot pot). If you reserve ahead there's a tiny room upstairs for about six people —a cosy place to have a hot pot in the winter!
A good restaurant owned by another friend is *Nada*. It's Kyoto-style food—but not formal like kaiseki. It's more a casual style of eating with many different dishes. It's not just meat and fish—there's many veggie dishes, so it's a good choice for vegetarians and vegans.
For fish and seafood a great place is *Kaikaya By The Sea*, which is also popular among visiting DJs. We always order the sashimi selection to start, and sometimes the tuna head.
And *Kiki* is an interesting bistro where they make everything with all kinds of fruits. Personally it's not to my taste but I guess it's good for girls as all of them there kept saying "oishii", "oishii" ("delicious").
When I really want barbecued meat, I go to *Yoroniku*. I don't eat meat at home, so sometimes I get the craving. I like their set menu.

Where do you take visiting DJs to show them the city?
They are usually too busy—they arrive, play, sleep, have dinner, then go home. But if they have time, it's nice to take a train out of Tokyo to Hakone or Izu for the onsen (hot springs). I'm from Asama Onsen in Matsumoto and I used to take a bath in a hot spring almost every day when I was a kid.

Do you have a favourite record shop?
I don't buy records but the ones the DJs go to are *Technique*, *Lighthouse Records* and *Disk Union*.

How about for gifts?
There's a great department store in Shibuya called *Tokyu Hands*. They have everything. You can easily spend two hours getting lost in there. Our visitors always go there to get souvenirs to take home.

Any favourite garden or park?
It's not a park but I love Icho Namiki Avenue. It's nice to walk there in autumn. Twenty years ago, the street was used in a popular TV drama, so many people know it. Apart from that, as you might know, Japanese people love cherry blossoms. If you're lucky enough to hit the right time—around end of March, beginning of April—you can see them in beautiful parks like *Aoyama Cemetery*, *Shinjuku Gyoen*, *Yoyogi Park*, or all along the Meguro River, for example. Another beautiful outdoor space is the *Teien Art Museum*. I like its architecture and it has a lovely garden.

Are there other museums you like?
Recently I've been really busy so I haven't had the time, but I used to really like the *Tokyo Photographic Art Museum* in Ebisu. Now it's been refurbished, so I'm sure it's even better.

Meguro River: one of many pink explosions when the cherry trees bloom and the city goes mad with delight

Toga
Harajuku

Sacai
Shinjuku

Pierre Hardy
Omotesando

You also studied fashion in London. How are Japanese designers today?

I liked the London fashion scene in the 1990s, which is why I went there... Of course we have Rei Kawakubo, Yohji Yamamoto and many famous ones. I don't spend money on fashion now... I met the designer of *Toga* at many parties for a long time. I never bought her clothes but I like the look. *Sacai* had Paradise Garage clothes last year which caught my attention. I like *Pierre Hardy* more than Manolo or Louboutin, and they have boots this season.

How will Tokyo be in ten years?

We have an ageing society with fewer children, so I'm not so optimistic about Tokyo and Japan in ten years. But for me, there's too many people in Tokyo right now, so fewer people would be more comfortable. As you know, the Olympic and Paralympic Games will be held in Tokyo 2020. Many people are expecting economic recovery, starting businesses or opening new shops, that's not bad for us. As we'll have many international visitors, it will give the Japanese people a good opportunity to mix with people from other cultures and broaden their vision.

Through the Pane

A showcase by Masataka Nakano

A master in finding the silent, secret side of the baffling metropolis, Nakano's 11-year project "Tokyo Nobody" caught the capital's busiest spots completely devoid of people. Here is an extract from his series "Tokyo Windows"

Yasuko Furuta, Fashion Designer
Thread Bare

The creator behind Toga graduated from ESMOD in Paris, taking her know-how back to Japan to start her celebrated fashion imprint. Deconstructed separates and reworked knitwear are Yasuko's calling card with her brand that puts as much effort into fabric research as it does confection, and has become a synonym for cool in Western fashionista land

"I create for a complex woman who can only live in chaos", says Yasuko. Long studio hours, a packed travel schedule and a son might have made life chaotic, but out of the complexity come some simple suggestions for embracing Tokyo—from relaxing picnics to festivals in a shrine

What's your Tokyo area like?
I live between Omotesando, Ebisu, and Shibuya stations. People tend to think it's not residential, but actually many families have lived here for a long time. But the area remains very urban and convenient.

What do you miss about Tokyo when you're away?
Soba noodles, Japanese broth… Simple, light food.

Tokyo restaurants can be less than welcoming for children. How do you manage with your son?
Recently, I've started to feel that my best bet are restaurants with strong personal colour. I've found they tend to allow children, especially if you visit early. Personally I like *Toramangen*, a Chinese place in Minami-Aoyama. My favourite, though, is to have a relaxing picnic in *Yoyogi Park*, where my son can play freely. A great place for lunch is *Eightablish*. It's a vegan café.

If you could create a uniform for the Tokyo woman, what would it be?
I actually designed a uniform for the staff of a cosmetic company once. It depends on the work that needs to be performed, but I think a uniform should be functional, but expressive, and provide its wearer with some options, not just one for men and another for women.

What's your favourite spot for people-watching in the city?
I think Shinjuku. The "Tori no ichi" festival held in the Hanazono Shrine during November is very fun.

What takes your mind off work?
Ordinarily, I go to yoga or bars and clubs. *Grassroots* is a great little DJ bar for music. *Liquid Room* is different from how it used to be since it moved to Ebisu but it still has great live acts. Upstairs in

Liquid Room is Kata Gallery—good for art. Or there's a new art complex in Roppongi called Complex665, which has great spots inside like *Tomio Koyama Gallery*.

Is Tokyo present in your designs at all?
No.

What is the one thing a style-conscious traveller should buy when in Tokyo?
Maybe nail clippers? Japanese nail clippers are amazingly sharp! Also, there are many socks shops that offer an incredible variety of socks, sold for ¥1,000 for three pairs.

Where would you take visiting friends shopping?
I almost never do, when I do it tends to be at vintage clothing stores, such as *Santa Monica* and *Pigsty* in Harajuku.

Are there any other local creators you follow?
I'm interested in Yomeiriland, a rap group comprising three women, and D.A.N., a band that plays club rock.

If you could change anything about your city, what would it be?
What really bothers me that many people here will not give up their seat on the bus or train for elderly or pregnant women, or others who need to sit. Too many people ignore others who clearly need help. I've even seen adults push elderly people out of the way to let their children sit.

What's the coolest souvenir you could send someone home with?
I like to buy local dishware wherever I travel. In Japan, I would recommend sake ware. The best place to find it are antique markets. Try the *Antique Fair* at *Hanazono Shrine* every Sunday. And look out for the dishware brand Shoji Morinaga.

Ebisu & Daikanyama
Upscale, In Tune

Sophisticated, gentrified, and perhaps a little baby-stroller heavy—yet Ebisu and its environs provide a superb wining and dining scene with some of Tokyo's best bars and clubs—all behind closed doors, of course

| Night | Nomikai Navigator |

Drinkers looking for a more grown-up alternative to the hectic Shibuya nightlife tend to head one stop along the Yamanote line to Ebisu. A sophisticated bar crawl might start at *Buri*, which has a unique selling point: its wide array of chilled sakes, all served in individual "one cup" glasses sourced from around the country. Around the corner, *Bar Tram* is a popular craft cocktail bar where you can also drink absinthe from ornate glass fountains, the way they did in the Belle Epoque. One block away find its sister shop, *Bar Trench*, which draws a slightly older crowd with a menu of 1920s and 1930s-style cocktails.

You can do more time travelling at *Bar Odin*, a revered cocktail temple equally famous for its range of antique spirits. If you need a caffeine fix between rounds, *Sarutahiko Coffee* stays open after midnight, and often has a lively street scene outside. As things wind down, a low-key nightcap beckons at *Bar Martha* (pictured), where customers are expected to speak sotto-voce so they don't drown out the music playing over the high-end Tannoy Autograph speakers.

• Ebisu, various locations, see Index p.60

Photos: 1) Julio Shiiki 2) Yoko Setoyama 3, 4) Julio Shiiki

| Night | **Stream Line**

Tokyo's club scene is on the up again following a successful campaign to amend an archaic law prohibiting all-night dance parties. There have been a few notable new arrivals recently: *Circus Tokyo* and *Contact* in Shibuya, and *Sankeys*, an outpost of the Manchester club, which took over the former home of Air in Daikanyama. Yet none have surpassed the sound system at *Unit* (pictured), which remains the club of choice for audio nerds. Parties are held most weekends, and range from underground techno to dub and hip-hop. It doubles up as an evening concert venue.
• Unit, Daikanyama, unit-tokyo.jp

| Culture | **Top Shots**

One of the most consistently interesting museums in the capital reopened in autumn 2016 after a lengthy renovation. *Tokyo Photographic Art Museum* usually has three shows at once, meaning on a given day you might see a retrospective for a big-name photographer, a group show of upcoming artists, and some historic selections from the rich archive. TOP stays open until 8pm on Thursdays and Fridays, and you can grab a drink afterwards at Brick End, a row of new cafés and bars on the concourse outside.
• Tokyo Photographic Art Museum, Yebisu Garden Place, Ebisu, topmuseum.jp

| Food | **Golden Bowls**

As any obsessive fan will tell you, ramen is much more than noodles in soup. That's especially true at *Suzuran*, which fancies up the fast-food staple. Selections can be ordered either as ramen or tsukemen dipping noodles, and they're all mighty fine: try the delicate shoyu-based "chuka" soba or the "kakuni" noodles, topped with slow-simmered pork belly that's meltingly soft. The 11-seater shop moved from its former Shibuya home to Ebisu a couple of years ago, and ditched its policy of playing nothing but Carpenters songs along the way. Count your blessings.
• Suzuran, Ebisu

Palace of the Word

With the DVD market dwindling, rental chain
Tsutaya has reinvented the bookshop instead.
Spread across three buildings, Tsutaya Books is
bookworm paradise. The vast selection of books
and periodicals is thoughtfully curated, with
small-press and English-language titles nestling
alongside major releases. The upstairs Anjin
lounge bar, where you can sip coffee and
cocktails while browsing a library of vintage
magazines, clinches the deal. It's the centrepiece
of a larger complex, *Daikanyama T-Site*, also
home to popular brunch spot Ivy Place.
• Daikanyama T-Site, Daikanyama, real.tsite.jp/
daikanyama

Shop It's in the Jeans

From cars to whisky, Japan has a rich tradition of
pinching foreign ideas and tweaking them to
perfection. The denim industry is no exception,
but if you can't make a pilgrimage to Kojima in
Okayama, a tour of Ebisu and Daikanyama is the
next best thing. Innovative Kojima-based brand
Kapital has three shops here, of which *Duffle with
Kapital* is the most eccentric. Osaka's *UES*
(pictured) sells more classically styled jeans,
jackets and flannel shirts at its Daikanyama
flagship store, while nearby *Okura* is devoted to
products coloured with traditional Japanese
indigo dyes, including the Blue Blue Japan brand.
• Ebisu, various locations, see Index p.60

Food Raw Deal

There are fancier—and pricier—places to get
sushi in Ebisu, where you can easily spend a
fortune on dinner for two with drinks. The long-
running *Sushi Matsue* can hold its own against
the best of them, but it hasn't forgotten its origins
as a dowdy local eatery. At lunchtime, it's a
genuine bargain—especially if you opt for the
weekdays-only "chirashizushi" rice bowl. Matsue
prides itself on a no-fuss, orthodox approach in
its cuisine; for less traditional sushi try sister
restaurant *Sushi Matsugen* down the street.
• Sushi Matsue, Ebisu, matsue.cc/ebisu; Sushi
Matsugen, Ebisu, sushi-matsugen.com

Food | Up Sticks

Yakitori (literally "grilled chicken") has come a long way. Until the mid-19th century the Japanese variety of Buddhism was taken to preclude the eating of meat. The Meiji government, in part to help breed stronger fighters, decided to ditch all that. The smell of cooking meat remained in poor taste, so for chicken, charcoal was used to temper the aroma. Yakitori was originally made from the muscly meat of birds killed in cock fights. After WWII, US breeds that were easy to mass-farm came onto the picture. In the 1950s, the skewers became the de facto food stuff for overworked salarymen on the way home—cheap, succulent, and perfect with cold beer. Nowadays a further mutation has taken place. A new wave of restaurants is offering a more upscale version, with premium chicken and gourmet offerings. *Kannonzaka Toriko* is a fine example. As well as classic sticks of "momo" (thigh) and "negi" spring onions, expect goodies like seared foie gras and liver mousse in an elegant, minimalist interior. Adventurous souls can even try "chouchu"—the unborn, partly fertilised egg. Expect jazz rather than J-pop, and a sommelier to help you pick a bottle from the sizeable wine list. The best seats are at the counter overlooking the kitchen.
• Kannonzaka Toriko, Ebisu, j-toriko.com/kannonzaka

A one-way ticket and an infatu-
ation with Japanese food
brought Robbie to Japan in
1980. His only plan—to leave
when he stopped enjoying it.
More than 35 years later he's
food writer at "The Japan
Times", regular contributor to
"The Guardian" and other
international media, and avid
updater of his blog "Tokyo
Food File". He's clearly not
going anywhere any time soon

Robbie Swinnerton, Food Writer

Plate Tectonics

Tempura, sukiyaki, tonkatsu, unagi, shabu-shabu, Japanese-style
steak, Japanese-style curry, yakitori, Korean broths, homemade pasta
and even killer French bistro fare... Let one of Tokyo's top food
writers guide you through the beautiful, delicious labyrinth. Warning:
you'll never want to find your way out again

What is the secret to being a happy gaijin in Tokyo?

The same secret as anywhere else in the world: infinite curiosity and a good sense of humour. But plenty of good sake certainly helps.

What's your neighbourhood and why?

I don't live in Tokyo. I live out on the coast, where I can see green hills, breathe good air, walk along a beach, gaze out to a horizon and meditate on sunsets behind Mount Fuji. That's my other "secret" to being happy in Tokyo.

Diving into the food scene, can you map out Japanese cuisine for us?

At its heart, Japanese food is all about rice and/or noodles. Rice is eaten at the end of the meal, and everything else is foreplay. High-end kaiseki restaurants serve multi-course meals that cover the full gamut of cooking styles in a single tasting menu. The obvious exception is sushi. Except it's not, because with sushi you're eating rice with every bite. A lot of people think sushi is about raw fish. Wrong. Sushi is about the rice—mixed with vinegar—underneath. If the rice is not perfect, the sushi is bad.

Speaking of sushi, how do we navigate what's out there?

Not all sushi is created equal, even in Japan. But you get what you pay for. At the top, expect 30,000 yen per head—which may not include sake. For this, expect superb seafood, the best at the peak of its season, cut in front of your eyes and fashioned with effortless skill into flawless nigiri.

Some high-end sushi restaurants can be stiff and formal, if the chef doesn't know you—and you don't speak Japanese. *Sawada* tends to be a quiet experience. But *Saito* has just the right balance of precision and informality. It's also slightly less expensive—which is why it's so popular, and virtually impossible to reserve. *Tokami* has a similar balance of quality vs. approachability; but because it only has one star—and not three like *Saito*—it's not so hard to book.

But even "ordinary" sushi in Tokyo is better than just about anywhere else in the world. A perfect example of a lower-to-mid-range chain is *Midori Sushi*. It's hard to spend over 10,000 yen a head, and it's usually half that, so the queues are long. You can't reserve, so arrive an hour before opening and wait. The Shibuya branch is among the best.

Japanese fish-love is famous, but there's an eel obsession too, right?

Leave it to the Japanese to transform the ordinary eel—that slippery, fatty, blue-collar fish—into a rich, satisfying, gourmet delicacy. This is done by steaming and grilling the fillets over charcoal, and seasoning with a sweet-savory sauce. Served over rice, it is so good. Especially at *Nodaiwa* or *Obana*, where they use wild eels rather than farmed.

The izakaya is Japan's own genre of pub-restaurant. What's the lowdown?

It's my favourite way of eating: order a beer and a few snacks; follow up with sake and more dishes; then a main or two, perhaps with shochu or awamori. Just as the mood takes you, and at your own pace: interspersing food and drink with increasingly vivid conversation that you'll probably forget in the morning. At some, the draw is they're cheap, cheerful and you can drink till they kick you out to catch the last train. Others offer more refinement, with sake and excellent quality dishes. Favourites in ascending order of quality and

Who said Michelin restaurants can't be playful? Bunny-eared gloves are just one of the surprises of the set menu at Den

Muto
Chuo-ku

Kamachiku
Bunkyo-ku

Kagari
Ginza

Rokurinsha
Chu-ku

Kuroki
Akihabara

Afuri
Ebisu

Henry's Burger
Daikanyama

Arms
Shibuya-ku

outlay are *Uoshin*—especially the Nogizaka one; *Kaikaya by the Sea*; *Namikibashi Nakamura*; and *Ajisen*.

And what's the best way to do tonkatsu—the Japanese schnitzel?
There are three names worth chasing down here: *Tonki*, for tradition; *Narikura* for flavour (and the longest lines); and *Butagumi*, for the gourmet range of pork varieties, in the superb setting of a venerable wooden house.

And how about tempura?
Like with sushi, the best places are those where you sit at counter and are served one morsel at a time, straight from the deep-frying wok to your plate. To get the hang, drop into a casual old-school place, like *Tsunahachi*, which won't stretch your budget. But to really understand why tempura is one

of the great genres of Japanese cuisine, head upmarket. At *Mikawa Zezankyo*, chef Tetsuya Saotome elevates deep-frying to an art form.

Can you introduce the noodle family?
There are three—or four, or ten—different styles. But I'll take three. Soba are buckwheat noodles —plebeian fare. They're simple but, when prepared in the traditional way, so satisfying. Especially when they're prepared in-house, rolled and chopped in front of you. To watch this, a visit to *Kanda Yabu Soba* or *Kanda Matsuya* is essential. To see soba in a more contemporary context, try *Muto* where chef Eisuke Muto incorporates handmade noodles into multi-meals of casual, and affordable, elegance.
Udon are handmade wheat noodles. *Kamachiku* is great at lunch, for a quick bowl of

Plate Tectonics

55

Trust the touch of chef Hideki Ishikawa at his eponymous kaiseki restaurant: three Michelin stars are not easy to come by

revivifying noodles. At dinner, settle in for sake and side dishes before the udon, giving a chance to appreciate the remarkable setting, a century-old brick storehouse with a beautiful garden view in the backstreets of atmospheric Nezu.

And finally, ramen. If you can get a filling bowl for 500 yen, why queue for an hour to eat at *Kagari*, *Rokurinsha*, *Kuroki* or *Afuri*? Because these are the new-wave places where you can see the future of ramen—not as a retro wave to the past but a creative salute to the future. Ramen purists might curl up their lips but there is a new cuisine hatching under our eyes.

Let's talk meat. Where can we get the best cuts? Or the best value?

You want wagyu? It's expensive. You want cheap meat? Really? Try *Henry's* for a great wagyu

burger—actually more like crushed wagyu between buns. For a more traditional burger, I do like *Arms*, near Yoyogi Park. Otherwise, stick with yakiniku for your meat injection. It's an alluring combination: beautifully marbled wagyu beef; charcoal in the grill; and a hip but casual setting. Plus at *Sumibi-yakiniku Nakahara*, young chef Kentaro Nakahara really knows his meat. Order his tasting set of five different beef cuts and prepare to be amazed by the overall richness of flavour—and subtle differences between each. But before grilling, order the tartare and three different sections of beef tongue. To close, the wagyu sushi: raw—not just rare—slices of the most succulent beef, over vinegared rice. Your mind will be blown.

Sushi Saito Minato-ku	**Any good food trucks, or markets?** Find a good selection of lunch

Sushi Saito
Minato-ku

Tacubo
Shibuya-ku

Casa Vinitalia
Minato-ku

Seirinkan
Nakameguro

Savoy
Minato-ku

Ostü
Shibuya-ku

Convivio
Shinjuku-ku

Pignon
Shibuya-ku

Chion Shokudo
Toshima-ku

Reikasai
Ginza

New York Bar
Shinjuku-ku

Gen Yamamoto
Minato-ku

Bar Trench
Ebisu

Bar High Five
Ginza

Omoide Yokocho
(Piss Alley)
Shinjuku

Golden Gai
Shinjuku

Any good food trucks, or markets?
Find a good selection of lunch trucks at *Tokyo International Forum*. But the best are at *Farmer's Market @ UNU*. There's always curry sellers and craft beer. Look for the smoked meats and even smoked eggs with handmade rice balls. A true food-truck artisan.

Which Tokyo chefs are hot right now?
All of the above. But most especially Zaiyu Hasegawa at *Den* for contemporary Japanese; Hideki Ishikawa at *Ishikawa* for upper-end; and *Kanda Matsuya* for traditional.

Is it true Tokyo's fancy restaurants often have great-value lunch deals?
Just about every restaurant does. Even some top-end sushi places offer set lunches for less than half the price of dinner. Three-star *Sushi Saito* is a good example. However not all do, such as Jiro.

Of course Tokyo also has worldwide cuisines. What are your tips?
Little Korea, north of Shinjuku in Okubo, has—unsurprisingly—great Korean. One of my old-time faves is *Matsuya*, where you sit on the floor, quaff makgeolli and eat rugged stews of pork bone and potato. For serious Italian, try *Tacubo* or *Casa Vinitalia*. For pizza, *Seirinkan* or *Savoy*, and for home-made pasta and great comfort food, *Ostü* or *Convivio*. Also, it's common knowledge Tokyo has some of the best high-end French cuisine around. Less obvious is it has great casual bistro food too. Track down brilliant, funky *Pignon*. Chinese: the spicy hotpots at *Chion Shokudo* are so authentic you could be in the heart of Sichuan. At the other extreme, at *Reikasai* you can dine on Imperial cuisine from the descendent of the Last Emperor's chef.

Any favourite sake at the moment?
Today my personal favourites are Shichihonyari, Tedorigawa, Tamagawa and Kaiun. Tomorrow it may well be quite different…

How would you plan a killer date?
Early evening cocktails in the famous *New York Bar* on the 52nd floor of the Park Hyatt Hotel; followed by dinner at Den; and après drinks at *Gen Yamamoto*.

More bars, from cocktail to dive?
Bar Trench (Ebisu) is a perennial favourite. *Bar High Five* in Ginza never fails. Nor for that matter do the late-night shochu cocktails on the funky side of the tracks in *"Piss Alley"* (*Omoide Yokocho*). And the all-night alleys of *Golden Gai*…

"Piss Alley" is a dense network of tiny restaurants. Any favourite stalls?
I learned to speak Japanese in the izakaya counters of Piss Alley—and usually forgot it again after too many drinks. My favourite places have changed hands, but there's always Kabuto, if you can get in. And Asadachi. It's best to have had a few drinks before you get there and not to ask what you're eating. Hint: it's not prime chicken. It's more likely to be pig gonads.

And where to drink in Golden Gai?
It doesn't matter where you end up in Golden Gai, it's always an experience. There's 270 little bars to choose from—well, in practice fewer, since quite a few only accept regulars—so just follow your nose. And your ears, too, since many of the bars specialise in specific music genres. I won't tell you my favourites or they'll get overrun and that would spoil it for everyone.

Books

Akira
• Katsuhiro Otomo, 1982-1990

Set in a post-apocalyptic Tokyo, this was one of the first manga series to be translated into English in its entirety. Together with its 1988 film adaptation it was fundamental in popularising the graphic art form outside Japan. The cyberpunk saga is a breakneck critique of despotic power, militarism and social isolation, as relevant today as ever.

Confessions of a Mask
• Yukio Mishima, 1949

Mishima was a giant in the arts who famously committed harakiri after a failed nationalist coup in 1970. But long before that, in his early twenties, he published his astonishing first novel—a first-person account of a homosexual boy failing to fit into the rigid, militaristic Japanese society.

Naomi
• Junichiro Tanizaki, 1924

This precursor to "Lolita" by the brilliant Tanizaki follows a salary-man attempting to westernise his young girlfriend. With its Japanese title literally meaning "A Fool's Love", the story mocks Japan's fascination with the West. The author narrowly missed out on the Nobel Prize, and wrote several seminal works including the influential essay on aesthetics, "In Praise of Shadows".

Films

Drunken Angel
• Akira Kurosawa, 1948

The first of Kurosawa's legendary collaborations with Toshiro Mifune presents a murky view of US-occupied Japan. But it's also a dramatic, humorous and moving story about an alcoholic doctor who forms an uneasy friendship with a small-time yakuza member in a disease-ridden Tokyo slum.

Tokyo Story
• Yasujiro Ozu, 1953

In Ozu's movies time slows, and epic emotions are launched with a simple gesture. Here, parents visit their grown-up kids in Tokyo only to find them too busy. Clashes of Japanese and Western culture, tradition and modernity are treated with the filmmaker's sweet subtlety.

Nobody Knows
• Hirokazu Koreeda, 2004

Four children are abandoned by their mother to look after themselves in a Tokyo apartment. The film premiered at Cannes, helping to establish Koreeda as one of the leading contemporary filmmakers of Japan.

Music

D.A.N.
• D.A.N., 2016

Spaced-out, mellow club rock: these three Tokyoites are riding a wave akin to that of Tame Impala or The xx, complete with drum machines and extra-disciplined bassist starter kit. That might explain why this debut LP speaks so fluently to the musical zeitgeist, regardless of language barriers.

Maki Asakawa
• Maki Asakawa, 2015

To have been a fly on the wall in one of those dark, smoky basement venues in the 1970s, where Maki Asakawa performed her sultry takes on blues, jazz and even Indian folk—cigarette in hand and melancholy on the brain. Enjoy with a measure of Nikka whisky.

Logic
• Logic System, 1981

Light years ahead, composer/programmer Hideki Matsutake's first album under this moniker is a seminal work in underground electronic music. Bleeps, blops and fat synth lines make this a brainy dancefloor teaser as much as a study in the quality of Japanese mastering techniques.

Also available from LOST iN

LOSTIN.COM

Index

1/ Chuo-ku

2/ Chiyoda-ku

3/ Minato-ku

Carhartt WIP
Store Tokyo

4-28-25
Jingumae
Shibuya-ku
Tokyo
150-0001

carhartt
WORK IN PROGRESS

www.carhartt-wip.com

Farmer's Market at UNU
United Nations University, 5-53-70 Jingumae
+81 3-5459-4934
farmersmarkets.jp
→ p.56 (F)

Gen Yamamoto
1F Anniversary Bldg, 1-6-4 Azabu-Juban
+81 3-6434-0652
genyamamoto.jp
→ p.57 (F)

Idea by SOSU
4-12-10 Jingumae
+81 3-3478-3480
→ p.16 (S)

Kyu Asakura House
29-20 Sarugakucho
+81 3-3476-1021
→ p.17 (C)

Minami Aoyama Shimizu-yu
3-12-3 Minamiaoyama
shimizuyu.jp
→ p.14 (O)

Mister Hoolywood
4-13-16 Jingumae
store.n-hoolywood.com → p.16 (S)

Mori Art Museum
Roppongi Hills, 6-10-1 Roppongi
+81 3-5777-8600
mori.art.museum
→ p.15, 17 (C)

Narisawa
2-6-15 Minamiaoyama
+81 3-5785-0799
narisawa-yoshihiro.com → p.16 (F)

Nezu Museum
6-5-1 Minamiaoyama
+81 3-3400-2536
nezu-muse.or.jp
→ p.14 (O)

Pierre Hardy
A103, 5-5-25 Minami-aoyama
+81 3-6712-6809
pierrehardy.com
→ p.35 (S)

Sato
Otomo Bldg, 4-1-4 Nishi-Azabu
+81 3-3797-0163
→ p.25 (F)

Savoy
1F M2K Stage, 3-3-13 Azabu-Juban
+81 3-3451-6699
savoy.vc
→ p.57 (F)

SuperDeluxe
3-1-25 Nishiazabu
+81 3-5412-0515
super-deluxe.com
→ p.11 (N)

Sushi Saito
1F Ark Hills South Tower, 1-4-5 Roppongi
+81 3-3589-4412
→ p.54, 57 (F)

The National Art Center, Tokyo (NACT)
7-22-2 Roppongi
+81 3-5777-8600
nact.jp → p.17 (C)

Tomio Koyama Gallery
2F Complex665, 6-5-24 Roppongi
+81 3-6434-7225
tomiokoyamagallery.com → p.47 (C)

Toramangen
7-8-4 Minamiaoyama
+81 3-3409-2291
kiwa-group.co.jp
→ p.47 (F)

Uoshin Nogizaka
9-6-32 Akasaka
+81 3-3405-0411
uoshins.com
→ p.55 (F)

Warayakiya
1F, 6-8-8 Roppongi
+81 3-5410-5560
→ p.11 (F)

Yaeca Home Store
4-7-10 Shirokane
+81 3-6277-1371
yaeca.com
→ p.16 (S)

Yoroniku
Luna Rossa, 6-6 Minamiaoyama
+81 3-3498-4629
→ p.34 (F)

4/
Meguro-ku

Cafe Eightablish
104, 1-7-11 Takaban
+81 3-6753-3316
eightablish.com
→ p.47 (F)

Chiyo-no-yu
1F Belle Maison Takaban, 2-20-3 Takaban
+81 3-3712-1271
tiyonoyu.com
→ p.14 (O)

Five Star Cafe
3-12-4 Kamimeguro
+81 3-3760-7028
golden-dining.com
→ p.23 (F)

Markaware
1-7-6 Kamimeguro
+81 3-5459-4181
marka.jp
→ p.14 (S)

Paradise Tokyo
1F Com's Forum, 2-3-2 Higashiyama
+81 3-5708-5277
wackomaria.co.jp
→ p.16 (S)

Seirinkan
2-6-4 Kamimeguro
+81 3-3714-5160
localplace.jp
→ p.57 (F)

Shibamatsu
1-11-16 Midorigaoka
+81 3-3717-5751
shibamatsu.com
→ p.23 (F)

Sushidokoro Shintanaka
2-5-10 Nakane
+81 3-3222-3978
→ p.16 (F)

Teien Art Museum
5-21-9 Shirokanedai
+81 3-3443-0201
teien-art-museum.ne.jp → p.34 (C)

Tractor
1-3-5 Nakameguro
+81 3-6303-3291
→ p.34 (N)

Tonki
1-1-2 Shimomeguro
+81 3-3491-9928
→ p.54 (F)

Vendor
1F Saito Bldg, 1-23-14 Aobadai
nonnative.jp
→ p.14, 16 (S)

Wacko Maria
1F Com's Forum, 2-3-2 Higashiyama
+81 3-5708-5277
wackomaria.co.jp
→ p.14, 16 (S)

5/
Shibuya-ku

Afuri
1-1-7 Ebisu
+81 3-5795-0750
afuri.com
→ p.56 (F)

Arms
5-64-7 Yoyogi
+81 3-3466-5970
maishoku.com
→ p.56 (F)

Bape
13-17 Udagawacho
+81 3-6415-6041
bape.com
→ p.10 (S)

Bar Martha
1-22-23 Ebisu
martha-records.com
→ p.48 (N)

Bar Odin
B1F, K-1 Bldg, 1-8-18 Ebisu
authenticbar.com
→ p.48 (N)

Bar Tram
2F Swing Bldg, 1-7-13 Ebisunishi
→ p.48 (N)

Bar Trench
Dis Bldg 102, 1-5-8 Ebisunishi
→ p.48, 57 (N)

Beams
15-1-19-8 Jinnan
beams.co.jp
→ p.16 (S)

Buri
1-14-1 Ebisunishi
→ p.48 (N)

Candy/Fake
18-4 Udagawacho
→ p.10 (S)

Yamaga Honten
1-5-9 Dogenzaka
+81 3-3461-3010
→ p.23 Ⓕ

Yogoro
1F Komatsu Bldg,
2-20-10 Jingumae
+81 3-3746-9914
→ p.16 Ⓕ

Yoshio Kubo
21-1 Udagawacho
yoshiokubo.jp
→ p.10 Ⓢ

6/
Shinjuku-ku

Antique Fair at
Hanazono Shrine
5-17-3 Shinjuku
→ p.47 Ⓞ

Convivio
1F Kamimura Bldg,
3-17-12 Sendagaya
+81 3-6434-7907
convivio.jp
→ p.57 Ⓕ

Disk Union
3-31-4 Shinjuku
+81 3-3352-2691
diskunion.net
→ p.34 Ⓢ

Golden Gai
1-1-7 Kabukicho
→ p.57 Ⓝ

Isetan
3-14-1 Shinjuku
+81 3-3352-1111
isetan.mistore.jp
→ p.16, 24 Ⓢ

Ishikawa
1F Takamura Bldg,
5-37 Kagurazaka
+81 3-5225-0173
kagurazaka-ishikawa.
co.jp → p.56, 57 Ⓕ

Narikura
1-32-11 Takadano-
baba
+81 3-6380-3823
→ p.55 Ⓕ

New York Bar
52F Park Hyatt Tokyo,
3-7-1-2 Nishishinjuku
→ p.16, 57 Ⓝ

Omoide Yokocho
(Piss Alley)
1-1-1 Nishishinjuku
→ p.57 Ⓕ

Sacai
3-14-1 Shinjuku
+81 3-3352-1111
sacai-info.blogspot.jp
→ p.35 Ⓕ

Tsunahachi
3-31-8 Shinjuku
+81 3-3352-1012
tunahachi.co.jp
→ p.55 Ⓢ

Yuma Koshino
5-24-2 Sendagaya
+81 3-3358-8293
yumakoshino.com
→ p.10 Ⓢ

7/ Koenji
& Kichijoji

Dachibin
3-2-13 Koenji-kita
+81 3-3337-1352
dachibin.com
→ p.8 Ⓢ

Dairakudakan
Kochuten
Favorite Kichijoji,
2-1-18 Kichijoji-
Kitamachi
+81 422-21-4984
dairakudakan.com
→ p.10 Ⓒ

Ghibli Museum
1-1-83 Shimorenjaku
+81 570-055-777
ghibli-museum.jp
→ p.20 Ⓒ

Harmonica Yokocho
1-31-6 Kichijoji-honcho
→ p.18 Ⓕ

Hayatochiri
3-4-11 Koenji-kita
→ p.19 Ⓢ

Hikari
3-48-2 Koenji-minami
→ p.19 Ⓝ

Inokashira Park
1-18-31 Gotenyama
→ p.20 Ⓞ

Los Apson?
4-3-2 Koenji-minami
losapson.net
→ p.20 Ⓢ

Niman Denatsu
1-7-23 Koenji-minami
den-atsu.com
→ p.19 Ⓝ

Sokkyou
3-59-14 Koenji-minami
+81 3-6304-9421
→ p.19 Ⓝ

Sound Studio Dom
4-25-7 Koenji-minami
+81 3-3318-3569
→ p.19 Ⓕ

Spank!
4-24-7 Koenji-minami
+81 3-3317-5690
spankworld.jp
→ p.19 Ⓕ

Suntrap
4-23-5 Koenji-minami
suntrap-tokyo.com
→ p.19 Ⓝ

Taisho
4-27-10 Koenji-minami
→ p.21

U.F.O. CLUB
B1F Harmony Bldg,
1-11-6 Koenji-minami
ufoclub.jp
→ p.19 Ⓝ

Violon
2-9-5 Asagaya-kita
meikyoku-kissa-
violon.com
→ p.19 Ⓞ

8/ Other

Chion Shokudo
B1 Miyagawa Bldg,
1-24-1 Nishi-
Ikebukuro, Toshima-ku
+81 3-5951-8288
→ p.57 Ⓕ

Eisei Bunko Museum
1-1-1 Mejirodai,
Bunkyo-ku
+81 3-3941-0850
eiseibunko.com
→ p.23 Ⓒ

Kamachiku
2-14-18 Nezu,
Bunkyo-ku
+81 3-5815-4675
kamachiku.com
→ p.55 Ⓕ

Little Soul Café
3-20-2 Kitazawa,
Shimokitazawa
+81 3-5454-9800
littlesoulcafe.com
→ p.33 Ⓝ

Mikawa Zezankyo
1-3-1 Fukuzumi,
Koto-ku
+81 3-3643-8383
→ p.55 Ⓕ

Nakano Broadway
5-52-15 Nakano,
Nakano-ku
nbw.jp/index.html
→ p.14 Ⓢ

Obana
5-33-1 Minamisenju,
Arakawa-ku
→ p.54 Ⓕ

Shirube
2-18-2 Kitazawa,
Shimokitazawa
+81 3-3413-3785
→ p.11 Ⓕ

INDIVIDUAL STYLE
UNITED SPIRIT

SHAMA DJ - WEARS JOYCE

HOUSE

Dr. AirWair
Martens
with Bouncing soles

#STANDFORSOMETHING
DRMARTENS.COM

BANANA YOSHIMOTO

TOKYO
ROMANSU

Tokyo Romance

Banana Yoshimoto

It's almost cherry blossom season, but maybe it will still be a while before you see anything but buds? I've never been to Tokyo before, you know.

I'd planned a trip to Tokyo to visit a Japanese friend—a woman I'd spent just a little time with in Paris. She and I had gone on a lot of walks together while we were there. We went to the Chapel of Our Lady of the Miraculous Medal, which the Japanese love, and which is full of pickpockets; we ate at countless cafés and bistros, and did taste tests of the pâtes de fruits at different shops; we made the rounds of the Louvre, went for soba, and kissed on the Pont Neuf like in movies.

"Here everyone's got masks on from the pollen," she said. "You shouldn't get your hopes up about seeing how pretty Japanese girls are."

We were talking on Skype, the screen freezing every so often, and she looked like a totally different woman from the uninhibited person I'd known in Paris. Wearing a white shirt, her face carefully made up, she seemed serious and proper, like some woman I didn't know who would never even think of going off on a trip somewhere alone.

This didn't make me uneasy, and I had no intention of leaning on her for everything while I was there, but I did feel a little sad. Already, time had passed.

"Anyway, I'll come pick you up at Narita in my car. I took the day off, so we can have fun together in Tokyo for the two days and a night you'll be here before you head off to Kyoto and Nara and wherever."

The words "have fun," coupled with the subtle smile that played on her lips, reminded me of how free she had been in Paris, and I started getting excited again. It's ridiculous how simple this stuff is. Naturally, I just smiled and nodded, giving no sign of what I was feeling.

"You'll be arriving early, so you'll want to check into your hotel first, right? So here's the question. What level of hotel will you be staying in?"

Ah, well, I decided to splurge a bit—I mean, it's not that much of a splurge, actually—and stay in the Palace Hotel, near the Imperial Palace.

"I'd say that's a good choice. Okay, so first we'll go there. There's this really nice old bar on the first floor, so we can round off day one with some of their famous martinis. Other than that, I think we should go to Asakusa. It's the same thing everyone does, but we can go see Sensoji Temple and Asakusa Shrine, which is right next door, because they're both really nice. When I was little, I used to go there for the lantern floating. We can walk around a while and buy some nice hand towels and so on, then go have sushi for lunch. There's this place called Bentenyama Miyako Sushi. It's really, really good. You like sushi, right?

"If you don't feel like sushi, there's a good soba place called Nagaura. The building it's in is really charming, and it's on a back street, so it feels kind of out of the way.

"After that we can walk around a little more, maybe look around this really unusual antique store called Tokyo Hotarudo. They've got lots of stuff from the Showa Period, things anyone who doesn't live in Japan would be wild about, I'm sure. Then snack time. There are a bunch of places we could go to. Naniwaya, Umezono, Umemura...

"That night, we can go back to the Marunouchi area and have dinner at the branch of Hantei there, or if you're feeling up to it we could go from Asakusa to Ueno and see Shinobazu Pond and Bentendo, and then eat at the original Hantei, in this cool three-story wooden building. Everyone loves their kushiage, no matter what country they're from. And they swap out the ingredients if you're a vegetarian or don't want meat or don't like fish or whatever. And then, since I don't recall you being the clubbing type, we'll finish up at the Royal Bar at the hotel."

Hold on, I said. You might as well be putting a spell on me, for all I understood. You're not giving me a sense of what any of those things are like, how fun, how good the food is.

"The fun is in breaking the spell." She laughed.

I don't think I could take hearing what you have planned for day two, I said. Besides, I'm worn out from writing it all down.

"I had an idea you might say that. Anyway, since I don't actually know you that well yet, I figured we could think about where in Tokyo we ought to go on the second day after our tour on the first. Should we go check out Roppongi? Or take a trip to Aoyama and Harajuku? Go walk around Shimokitazawa and Sangenjaya, or sleep in and go stroll around Kitanomaru Park before heading over to Jinbocho to hit the bookstores and cafés? There are all kinds of possibilities. Obviously, some options are good if you've got some money to spend, and others let you have fun without spending much at all."

She was smiling as she spoke.

The one thing I understood was that Tokyo has all kinds of different faces to show you, and that I could have any sort of experience as long as I had a definite sense of what I wanted. I could see, too, that she loved good food, and loved her life, and living in Tokyo. And that was good enough for me.

Born in Tokyo in 1964, Banana Yoshimoto won fame with her first novella "Kitchen" in 1987. Her works have been translated and published in more than 30 countries

Translated by Michael Emmerich
Illustration by Jonathan Niclaus

On The Road

The perfect companion for your city trip.

Access thousands of handpicked locations from your phone.
Download our free app on lostin.com/app

@lostincityguides